contemporary asian
BEDROOMS

Chami Jotisalikorn and Karina Zabihi
photos by Luca Invernizzi Tettoni

PERIPLUS

Published by Periplus Editions with
editorial offices at 130 Joo Seng Road
#06-01 Singapore 368357

ISBN 0 7946 0180 4
Printed in Singapore

Distributed by:
North America, Latin America and Europe
Tuttle Publishing, 364 Innovation Drive,
North Clarendon, VT 05759-9436, USA
tel: (802) 773 8930; fax: (802) 773 6993
email: info@tuttlepublishing.com
www.tuttlepublishing.com

Asia Pacific
Berkeley Books Pte Ltd, 130 Joo Seng Road
#06-01/03, Singapore 368357
tel: (65) 6280 1330; fax: (65) 6280 6290
email: inquiries@periplus.com.sg
www.periplus.com

Japan
Tuttle Publishing, Yaekari Building, 3F,
5-4-12 Osaki, Shinagawa-ku,
Tokyo 141-0032
tel: (813) 5437 0171; fax: (813) 5437 0755
email: tuttle-sales@gol.com

contemporary asian bedrooms:
the new comfort zone

The bedroom, long cherished as the personal space where we withdraw from the world, is the one part of the house that is free from the demand to be dressed up and paraded for public display. Guests are entertained in the living and dining rooms, whereas the bedroom remains unbreached as the sanctum sanctorum where we retire to sleep, rest, and recharge our batteries before facing the world again at the start of each new day. Ironically, though we spend half our lives in the bedroom, most of it is spent with our eyes shut, so it's no surprise that the precious bedroom often gets the least attention from busy homeowners, because the occupants themselves get scant time to appreciate the full potential of the design directions that lie dormant in it.

But more and more, the bedroom is basking in the rising heat of growing design attention. Across the region, bedrooms are making a style shift from the predictable formula of blocky bed inside a boxy cube, to suites of dreams that incorporate open bathrooms, personal massage rooms, miniature movie screens, and much more.

Why the new approach to sleeping? In fact, it can be surmised that the contemporary Asian bedroom is exploring new levels of creativity and luxury not so much in response to the way we sleep, but more in response to the way we are reacting to the world around us. With the increasing unpredictability of events in the world and our lessening ability to control outside forces, or avoid their sudden impact on our daily lives, we look increasingly toward our interior worlds as a place of stability and security. Because of its unique function as a room that is not meant for public use or as communal space, the bedroom has become a place where we are drawn to hibernate; a nest where we can relish in the comfort of our own private space.

What we see in the following pages of *Contemporary Asian Bedrooms* are the exciting new ways that designers and homeowners are putting more creative and increasingly customized spins on the role of the bedroom, elevating it to new dimensions from more than just a sleeping space and seeing it emerge as zen sanctuary, entertainment zone, personal art gallery, pampering retreat, and more.

Looking at the bedrooms created and coveted in the most stylish homes and hotels in Southeast Asia today, the common thread that runs throughout is that they all conform to the western concept of the bedroom. Even in the cases where the rooms have Asian design themes, they tend to be just that—themes that pick up on décor elements of say, Japanese or Balinese style, but still conforming to the western characteristics of a walled room with an elevated bed and en suite bathroom. Even in homes where an ethnic style prevails throughout the house, the bedroom remains stubbornly western—synonymous with modern—because western bedrooms come equipped with all the mod-cons that traditional Southeast Asian bedrooms lacked. In contrast to European sleeping traditions, where the bed is raised from the floor to avoid discomforting chilly draughts, tropical Asians did all their living, including sleeping, on the floor. Traditional bedding consisted of reed mats which, unlike fabric, does not induce perspiration, thus keeping the body cool and dry in the torrid equatorial heat. Shaped by a different way of living, traditional Southeast Asian bedrooms required nothing more than a reed mat, a mosquito net, and a basket for storing personal belongings. Such spartan arrangements were well suited to the rudimentary requirements of agrarian-based, olden-time living, but are disastrously out of sync with the need for more convenient creature comforts in contemporary urban life.

Perhaps the most important tropical sleeping item is the mosquito net—as anyone who has suffered the relentless attacks of the climate's pestilent swarms will readily agree. With the influx of colonial Europeans, the habit of sleeping in raised beds came into practice, along with European-style canopy beds which seemed custom-designed for hanging mosquito nets. To this day the alluring image of the wooden canopy bed shrouded in wispy white mosquito netting remains the enduring icon of romantic tropical living—and a feature that unfailingly lures tides of guests to Asian resort hotels.

Fast forward from colonial times to the present day. The dreamy mosquito net has become all but obsolete in the modern world of highrise apartment living. With Southeast Asian living tastes turning to western-style apartments and all their comforts, the ubiquitous air-conditioner has banished the need for open-air netting. But on these pages, we see that there remains an insistent craving to cling to the romantic notion of the things past. The mosquito net, or the idea of it, is still used as a décor element in even the most contemporary urban homes, as shown in the ultra-modern Sky Villas condominiums in Bangkok where elegant white bed curtains add infinite grace to a staid room (page 104). The mosquito net also makes its appearance in contemporary tropical resorts, as seen at The Club at The Legian Bali (page 56) as well as Villa Ylang Ylang in Bali (page 58).

Contemporary Asian Bedrooms shows us one of the most popular bedroom concepts sweeping the region today—the bedroom-cum-bathroom, where barriers between bed and bath have been broken down and replaced with versatile sliding wall panels. Examples of this include a Bangkok condominium designed by Singaporean firm APC (page 94), the sliding wooden shutters at Phuket's Twin Palms Hotel, also designed by APC (page 106), and a contemporary oriental bedroom at Golden Nakara villas designed by P49 Deesign (page 24).

In the contemporary cool bedrooms from Singapore to Bangkok, we see varied interpretations of the concept of bedroom as minimalist cocoon, with a white-on-white theme creating ethereal capsules where time and space seem suspended inside pristine white shells. It's as if the absence of color is a metaphor for a mental purity that detoxes the mind and spirit from the disorienting kaleidoscope of the frenetic world outside.

The TV has become a ubiquitous presence in every bedroom. Once camouflaged inside ornamental cabinets, flat-screen TVs are now wall-mounted opposite the bed, thus lightening the room's clutter. The bedroom as personal entertainment zone reaches new heights in a Bangkok bedroom designed by DWP Cityspace (page 102), where the bed comes equipped with a built-in, retractable movie screen and sound system—fully automatic, of course.

One of the most interesting trends gradually creeping onto the scene is the bedroom as spa suite. Inspired by the fantasy spa interiors seen in the regions' luxurious spa resorts, homeowners are now realizing they can replicate the same comforts in their own homes—and why not bring that fantasy home with you? This approach is seen in a Bangkok luxury villa designed by P49 Deesign (page 108), where the master bedroom suite incorporates a personal massage room, complete with professional massage table, scented oils and towel rack within arm's reach.

top left Muslin drapes inject romance and nomadic chic to this bedroom in Bali.
top right Sleek-and-simple continues to be a popular choice, as seen in this bedroom in Bangkok.
opposite top The lavish red drapes and bedspread coupled with modern Chinese art give this Singapore bedroom an alluring sensuality.
right Lighting reflected upward from the ceiling beams creates a soft, dramatic effect in the bedroom, heightened by burnt-orange walls.
far right The cheeky humor of the artwork adds a refreshing note to this bedroom at Downtown Apartments in Bali.

What fuels this inspiration to reach for greater dimensions in today's bedrooms? The impact of travel plays on enormous role. With the ease and frequency of global travel today, people now spend more time in hotel rooms, and are exposed to an incredibly diverse variety of bedroom design and comfort levels. Thanks in part to the new wave in boutique hotels and design hotels that create fantasy worlds for people to sleep in, designers and homeowners have become increasingly influenced by what they see and experience, and are seeking to replicate these exotic styles and sumptuous comforts in the home, so that living large is part of their daily life—rather than an expensive treat sporadically sampled in another time zone.

The open bathroom concept seen in so many new bedrooms came directly from resort design. The semi-outdoor bed-and-bath suite is another resort concept that's migrated into urban apartments. In one Bangkok penthouse (page 82), the owners, inspired by their holidays in Bali, created a semi-outdoor bedroom suite with a completely open shower and bathtub on their bedroom balcony. At the push of a button, a sliding glass panel opens, and closes when the occupants require private, air-conditioned comfort.

Apart from borrowing hotel design concepts for their homes, some travelers bring the hotel bed back home with them; some hotels sell their down pillows, 400-thread count sheets and extra thick mattresses to guests who can't relinquish the comforts of hotel luxury. After all, isn't a great hotel suite the height beautiful living?

left Wall-mounted lamps free up the space on the nightstand, offering more space in small apartments.
above left Comfy sofa by day, extra bedding by night, the versatile day bed—like this one in the Evason Resort in Hua Hin, Thailand—is a popular feature in many modern Asian bedrooms.
above right This simple bedroom in the Phuket Yacht Club is a perfect example of the unisex, monochromatic look of today's bedrooms.

Among the designers making an impact in hotel design these days, we show in this book the work of Kathryn Kng, Singaporean designer of The Metropolitan Hotel Bangkok and other top resorts around the region, and the Singaporean firm APC, who designed the boutique hotel Twin Palms Phuket as well as a number of luxury homes and condominium projects around the region. With people becoming entranced by hotel rooms and hiring designers and architects to replicate the same style in their homes, there is cross fertilization between hotels and private homes, as well as the chance for designers to experiment with new concepts in one category and then continue reinterpreting them in the other category.

When it comes to the look and mood in contemporary Asian bedrooms, we see that homeowners love to create bedrooms that embody specific decor themes. Seen in this book are a variety of thematic bedroom concepts, such as the contemporary Thai bedroom at The Sukhothai Bangkok, fully appointed in luxurious Thai silk (page 44); the Japanese tatami room seen in a Bangkok penthouse complete with tatami flooring and *shoji* screens (page 36); varied interpretations of the minimalist zen bedroom; the ethnic bedroom covered with tribal textiles ranging from a Navajo blanket on the wall to Afghan rug on the floor (page 62); variations on the Italian minimalist bedroom, and many more. Of these, the most recurring and reinterpreted theme is the zen bedroom. Its popularity is only natural; the zen concepts of simplicity and purity are perfect expressions of the tranquility we seek in the room where we retire to unwind and rest at the end of the day.

"Whisper, don't shout," is the intended message in the unobtrusive bedroom palette, which encourages us to retreat, relax and repose. Say goodbye to anything chintz, baroque or rococo. The frilly, feminine bedroom has been pushed aside in favor of the unisex bedroom. Today's bedrooms seem to

shun the two extremes between flagrant florals and macho masculine, and instead flourish in the safety of neutral colors, middle-of-the-road monochromes. Single tones, blocks of color and textures are in. When bright color does appear in these bedrooms, it is restricted to a single color theme, and is executed in warm tones on soft materials, avoiding anything that looks or feels too loud or hard.

With the bed the star of the show, the challenge is to transform the basic boxy mattress into the cradle of our

above Big, bold headboards like this gold-leaf example add drama and flair to even the most conservative room, and are now seen in myriad styles ranging from silk to suede in new Asian bedrooms.
top The contemporary bedroom reveals the new global chic, mixing an Italian sofa and lamps with a 19th century Chinese cabinet and 3rd century Vietnamese temple bell.
right With the sliding doors closed, bright, warm colored cushions paired with yet another variation of the mosquito net transform this bedroom into a cozy and personal space.

dreams. Headboards are springing out in a big way. Padded, paneled, covered in soft and silky fabrics, a beautiful headboard immediately adds drama and elegance to the plainest room. Some stunning new interpretations are seen in the white leather headboard by Index Design Singapore (page 122), and a sumptuous faux fur and Thai silk headboard by kzdesigns in Singapore (page 114).

No longer just a mattress on legs, bed design has transcended the basic boxspring into full-fledged bed systems. Minotti and B&B Italia are two of the dominant brands that offer all-in-one bed units that incorporate bed, headboard, and

left Roller blinds are the definitive choice for modern bedrooms. A Chinese scroll table and Japanese screen accentuate the clean space.
top The combination of hard terrazzo and soft *merbau* wood frame the bed and make it the main feature of the bedroom at The Balé.
above The curving lines of the frosted glass wall, echoed in the B&B Italia bed and Philippe Starck lamps temper the starkness of this futuristic bedroom.

side tables in one solid unit, as seen in Domus condominiums in Bangkok (page 94). The bed becomes a self-contained world, a cozy nest where its occupants can work, email, eat, read, watch TV, and when all else is done, eventually sleep.

With the bed taking on an alter ego as a bigger and better sofa, additional backing comes in the form of layers of pillows, padded with layers of throw cushions and the occasional bolster for added support. The new cushion textures are anything soft and fuzzy, with the emphasis on nubby, shaggy, and fluffy —the kind of fabrics you want to cuddle up to (mostly because of their resemblance to teddy bears!). Having crept into the boudoir via the living room, leather is ruling the roost as the sexy new texture in the bedroom. With textile technology offering fantastic faux substitutes to traditionally delicate suede and expensive fur, we now see a celebration of headboards, bed frames, cushions, duvets, bed-spreads, and throws, and even floor tiles covered in the full range of leather-like materials that mimic the buttery softness of suede, the exotic patterns of lizard, and the snuggly luxury of fur.

Seen in its myriad interpretations, the contemporary Asian bedroom has become a place where we can mentally relax, lounging in front of the TV, sunken in a cocoon of cushions; it caters to our bodily comforts with en suite bathtubs and personal massage chambers; it takes on the qualities of a spiritual retreat when shrouded in puritanical white. Whether entertainment complex, pampering suite or meditation chamber, the bedroom's new identities reflect the ways we seek physical and psychological relief in our private space. Today's Asian bedroom is not just about sleeping—it's about creating a personal comfort zone of security in our uneasy world.

above Organic materials and dark earth tones give inviting warmth to this zen bedroom in Bangkok.
right The mosquito net, or the idea of it, as expressed in these wispy bed draperies remains a romantic presence in contemporary bedrooms throughout Asia.

italian lullaby Italian contemporary rules the roost in this Bangkok bedroom designed by Vitoon Kunalungkarn of IAW. The large house calls for distinctive pieces of furniture that can stand on their own without being lost in the expansive space.

above The new global chic sees Italian contemporary paired side by side with antique Asian. The white Minotti chair is designed by Rodolfo Dordoni and standing lamp, by Cassina. Beside them stands a rare antique Thai medicine chest from Singhburi, its drawers still labeled with the names of the ancient Thai herbs they once contained, in the original Thai writing.

left A big room requires a great big bed. This one is by B&B Adio designed by Paolo Diva, with bedside lamps by Flos Romeo Moon. Though European design dominates, the east-meets-west aesthetic is present with antique Tibetan rugs. Sliding panels replace traditional curtains along one wall that opens onto an outdoor personal massage deck.

fit for a king "Villa Umah di Beji" in Bali means "house on a sacred spring" and the main theme running through this opulent villa is water. Nestled round the villa are these majestic yet intimate bedrooms.

left The enormous seven-foot bed is flanked by a *jati* wood counter with beaten copper edging and *mahoni* columns. Chinese-inspired antiques from all over Indonesia add a dramatic note. The central placing of the bed allows access to the adjoining desk behind it. Traditional Balinese checks get a modern makeover in the cushions.

above The bedroom benefits from impressive Alang Alang ceilings. Mosquito netting, essential for tropical climates, can be beautiful as well as practical, as evidenced by these romantic drapes enclosing the bed.

whitening heights
Designed by Bangkok architectural firm Boughey and Associates, this master bedroom in a Pattaya weekend home is an ethereal escape from the jarring fracas of Bangkok life.

left A cozy dressing room and vanity area are created by a diagonal wall. The high corner window brightens up the alcove with natural sunlight. The painting by Chinese artist Wallase Ting was bought in Hong Kong years before this house was built.
opposite An all-white scheme was born from the need for a glamorous, yet fuss-free house. Having lived surrounded by color and chaos in their daily lives for years, the owners wanted to experiment with living in a color-free space in their holiday residence. Cathedral height and tall windows lend celestial grandeur to this triangle-shaped room. A simple travertine headboard and wall-mounted lamps keep the space pristine.

asiatic blooms   Another take on contemporary Asian chic is seen in this bedroom created by P49 Deesign for Golden Nakara villas in Bangkok. The Asian aesthetic is energized by a blaze of colors evoking the brilliant hues of tropical flowers.

left Bathroom merges with bedroom via sliding glass panels—a concept popularized by resort design and now becoming de rigueur in homes. The bathroom is accessed through the walk-in closet and dressing room, seen on the left. The versatile day bed can be used as chaise longue, sofa or extra bed, depending on how you dress it.

right The view from the bathtub shows the full impact of the dramatic four-poster bed, framed by the dark wood wall which makes an elegant headboard, complete with moody alcove lighting. The bed's vertical lines provide the illusion of height, balanced by the horizontal element in the low side drawers that resemble Asian altar tables.

below A super-sleek cabinet hides the ubiquitous TV. The simple but delicate elegance of the dark wood desk gives zen-like balance to the space.

modern olympia The absence of any overtly Balinese ornamentation "maximizes the quality of the space," according to architect Antony Liu who designed the starkly beautiful villas at The Balé in Nusa Dua, Bali.

left The villas are designed in such a way that the bedroom, living room, bathroom and outdoor swimming pool are all interconnected. The monochromatic color scheme and terrazzo used for the floors and platform of the bed ensure the modern crispness the architect was after. What is particularly striking in the room is the *merbau* window that frames the bed. The double blinds—one inside the other—add to the idea of a picture-frame headboard. With no clear boundaries between the outside and inside, Antony Liu has artfully combined the modern and the traditional with a Balinese Alang Alang roof for the interior of the villa and a concrete flat roof for the outdoor patio.

above The serenity of the outside lounge area is accomplished by the skillful juxtaposition of Paras Jogja for the walls and exposed white plaster for the columns offset by the graceful lines of the furniture. The architectural team, who designed all the outdoor furniture, was inspired by the "modern and simple character" of the hotel.

a room for all reasons The owners of this house in Singapore designed by Sim Boon Yang of Eco-id Architects wanted a huge master bedroom because "in the evenings the whole family gathers there."

above The sumptuousness of the room is augmented by the teak wall where a 13th century Cambodian carving dominates the recessed and lit niche. The armchairs and sofa were custom made in Hong Kong.

right The chocolate tones of the bed—custom made in Thailand—are enhanced by this lacquer tray and silver vase from Club 21.

left A sleek wardrobe unit separates the bathroom from the rest of the room. It also conceals the audio/video equipment and leads to an office upstairs. Rotating louvered slats let in light. A day bed set in the window frame is large enough for all three of the owners' children.

romantic wanderlust   The bedrooms in Anneke Van Waesberghe's house on the edge of the Campuhan River in Ubud, Bali, hark back to the days of the deluxe safari tents of Hollywood movies of the '30s and '40s.

left In this bedroom, romance with a capital "R" is the order of the day. Pure white linens, layers of voile curtains and gauze panels behind the bed evoke a heady sensuality. With the room completely open to the elements, the surrounding nature becomes an inherent part of the space.

opposite In this sumptuous bedroom, Anneke shows that white need not be a sanitized and cold color, but instead can be restful and welcoming. The combination of dark wood floors, voile curtains used as "wallpaper," and floor-to-ceiling translucent drapes hugging the bed provide a dreamy quality to the room. Interesting details such as the "tent" wardrobe and tall candle holders imbue a nomadic touch.

white nights Big, bold space and bright white light are the key elements that create a pristine, luxury dream room in this Bangkok bachelor's bedroom designed by Architects 49. The effect is a stunning bedroom that is both sophisticated and serene.

left A floating bed by B&B Italia is the room's centerpiece, flanked by Philippe Starck bedside lamps. On the far wall, a pastel sofa from Cassina and a barely-there standing lamp from Artimede whisper understated elegance.

above A Corbusier reclining chair is reflected in high style in this Italian mirror from Fiamm.

oriental dreams In this Bangkok penthouse, a contemporary Asian concept is interpreted differently in two bedrooms—contemporary Thai in the master bedroom and contemporary Japanese in the guest room.

above Asian luxury comes from the shimmering Thai silk walls, silk bedspreads and silk bedside lamps from Jim Thompson, while the fantastic polished copper mirror provides an eclectic touch of Italian palazzo.

right While adding drama, the elegant overhead beam design was in fact the functional solution to the problem of how to conceal an uneven ceiling. To avoid the rustic look normally associated with exposed beams, they were made smooth and sharp, while lighting is reflected back onto the ceiling from the beams to create a softer effect and avoid harsh downlighting. The spacious bed was custom made to fit in with the proportions of the large room.

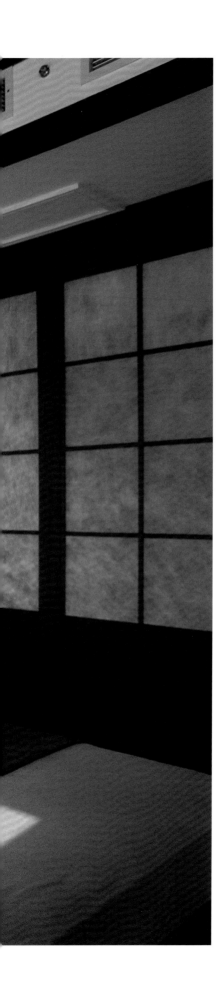

above The dark wood ceiling and window panes styled like classic sliding doors evoke the tranquil elegance of a Japanese house.
left A Japanese theme was chosen for penthouse guest room because the owners were attracted to the spare, zen simplicity that fit in with the modern Asian aesthetic. The rice paper lantern, a low bed and *shoji* screen doors incorporate the classic features of Japanese style; monochrome tones were selected in a range of beiges and browns to give an overall effect of subdued calm. Japanese tiles bearing different patterns above the bed are from a famed ceramics studio in Tokyo.
right Real tatami matting gives bare feet the feel of authentic Japanese flooring.

brilliant blue yonder   Using a blue color palette, these rooms designed by Abacus
Design for Sky Villas condominiums in Bangkok show how blue can spell refreshing,
in one room and relaxing, in another.

left The combo of bright white and brilliant blue brings an exhilarating energy reminiscent of sky and sea. The four-poster bed's sharp, clean lines are sleekly modern in black. Enormous twin mirrors flanking the bed give the small space extra dimension.

above In the narrow spare room, a wide day bed is custom-fitted into an alcove facing a TV. With a quick change of linens, the room is converted from play den by day to guest room by night.

masculine glamor   Deep colors, shiny surfaces and a departure from the conventional layout are the hallmark of slick urban bachelor pads, as seen in this bedroom designed by DWP Cityspace in Sky Villas Bangkok.

above The bathroom, located behind the bed, is conveniently accessible by doors on both sides of the bed. The bathroom's frosted glass sliding doors are a smaller version of the bedroom doors, and lets in natural light.
right Leather enters the bedroom again. The unexpected feel of buttery tanned leather floor tiles gives the feet a luxurious treat. A conventional hinged door is replaced by ultra-cool frosted glass double panels that slide back, opening the bedroom area into the living room and making the small apartment seem bigger. The bed is loaded with layers of comfort, ranging from jumbo-sized pillows to shaggy throw cushions and a faux fur throw. An additional layer of cushioning comes from the removable padded headboard.

wrap effect   The all-in-one bed system consisting of bed frame, headboard and nightstands in one unit is the hot new look in bed design. Kathryn Kng takes it one step further at The Metropolitan Bangkok.

above and opposite These custom-designed headboards wrap around the room and extend to the bedside bench seating. With seating thus relegated to the sidelines, the smooth, soft beauty of the *makha* wood floor stands out, enhanced by the subtle uplighting from behind the dark wood headboard unit. Below the lotus painting by Thai artist Natee Utarit, bendy Italian lamps offer personalized lighting for reading between Italian sheets. The Thai silk bed covers are designed by Kathryn Kng.

right East meets west in the corner where a parchment pendant lamp from Italy looks perfect on top of an Asian lacquer tray.

silken splendor The ultra-luxurious garden suite at The Sukhothai Bangkok—the work of Singapore-based architectural firm Kerry Hill—is no newcomer to the style scene, but remains the benchmark of contemporary design.

left The opulence of pure Thai silk shimmering from virtually every surface brings out the feeling of luxury that simply can't be replicated by lesser fabrics. Furniture designed by Chantaka Puranananda of Pure Design is also upholstered in Thai silk. The TV on a custom-designed swivel base that rotates 360 degrees is a mod-con unique to The Sukhothai.

above A luxurious night's sleep in a canopy bed surrounded by the decadence of pure Thai silk is an indulgence best accompanied by breakfast in bed.

a space for silence

The cachet of Albano Daminato's bedroom in the Singapore apartment he designed lies in the use of multi shades of white and cream and "the way the changing light from the outdoor spaces and sea plays on this."

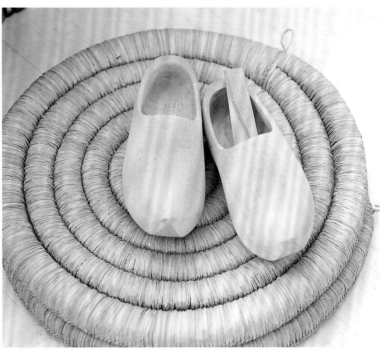

above left The G.O.D shop in Hong Kong is well known for its eclectic and stylish furnishings. This clothes hanger is a perfect vehicle for Albano's collection of throws and blankets from India.

above Dutch wooden clogs that the designer found in Chinatown provide an appealing counterpoint to woven mats from Japan.

left A uniquely shaped wooden box makes an eye-catching storage solution for sweaters.

opposite Albano's starting point for the design of the bedroom was to keep the space in front of the windows facing the sea open and free of any furniture, to create "a space for silence and tranquility." The polka-dotted paper lantern designed by Isamu Noguchi makes a singularly bold and fun statement.

radiant rouge   These striking scarlet rooms designed by Abacus Design for Sky Villas condominiums in Bangkok swing to the extreme end of the color spectrum and reveal how red can convey two different moods—mature luxury and youthful chic.

above A structural pillar in the middle of this room created awkward alcoves. The solution was to cover the pillar with mirrors and build a platform around it to unify the two alcoves. One side forms a niche for a bed; the other side, a window seat with a bird's eye view of the city below.
right Gold-leaf on red painted wood is a creative alternative to classic Thai lacquer work.
left This twin bedroom takes the feeling of expensive comfort from the plush interiors usually seen in five-star hotel rooms. Dramatic impact comes from the red theme—a sparkling red and gold Thai-style wall panel flanked by burgundy fabric headboards. A Chinese-style cabinet conceals the TV. The door is covered in real lotus leaves treated with a bronze color finish.

top Shaggy is the trendy texture in area rugs, like this red number made of Thai cotton. Leather boxes are chic solutions for concealing unsightly clutter.

above Seating is sculpture in this sinuous plastic desk chair. Built on a swivel stand, the full-length mirror can rotate up to 180 degrees.

right The curved window forms an alcove for lounging, defined by an area rug, seats, and artwork by Bali-based American artist Symon. The wooden headboard doubles as a mini-art gallery showcasing works such as this funky series executed on rice sacks by Australian artist Andrew Wellman.

city style Designed by Philosophy for State Tower condominiums in Bangkok, this master bedroom and guest room reflect a youthful, contemporary style that suits the tastes and lifestyle of urban professionals where compact quarters don't.

above The issue of fitting furnishing into a compact condo space is solved with a tabletop ledge running the full length of the room—it doubles as a desk on one end, vanity counter on the other end, and TV stand in the mid section.

right The use of leather signals contemporary cool in this bedroom, seen here in a wide headboard made of faux suede. The headboard material is repeated in the bed frames, pulling the whole look together. Faux pony skin and suede-like cushions complete the hip hotel feel.

club drama Architect Shinta Siregar and interior designer Jaya Ibrahim designed The Club at The Legian in Bali to be a comfortable space in keeping with the surroundings, and also a space that "allows you to escape into yourself."

left The interplay of the Alang Alang roof, terrazzo floor and centrally positioned bed creates a natural harmony in the villa. The bedspread is a handspun, hand-dyed and handwoven fabric from a village in East Java. The design was inspired by the Scottish tartan, modernized by Burberry, and reinterpreted by Wieneke of NILAM.

above There is a graceful fluidity between the spaces. The villas are designed so that there is no separation between the interior and exterior, as Jaya Ibrahim explains, "I am always concerned about the experience one gets looking at every single square centimeter of the building, from within and without, and from every possible angle."

nocturne in leather Leather is making its way from the living to the bedroom. The Bangkok bedroom of Vichien Chansevikul and Michael Palmer, partners in the export décor firm Leather Paragon, reveals a soft new look for nighttime leather.

left A marshmallow-soft white pleather armchair sourced from a local department store paired with real suede cushions from Leather Paragon offers seating you can sink into at the end of a long day.

below This tooth-shaped tray table covered with exotic mock lizard leather in fire engine red is just one funky item from Leather Paragon. Giraffe and zebra patterned candles add warmth to the room's solid blocks of color.

opposite While leather in the living room tends to take on a slick, masculine look, it takes on softer textures and colors more suited for slumber time in the bedroom. The master bedroom is divided into a study area and bedroom area, separated by a small sitting area. The black pouf in woven leather is from Leather Paragon, as is the cube covered in blonde mock lizard, which doubles as a side table or a stool with the addition of a cushion seat.

room with a view Danielle Mahon was inspired by "the poetry of the different Aman hotels and The Legian," when she designed the master bedroom of Villa Ylang Ylang in Bali for herself and her husband.

above Luscious silk curtains entice you into the master bedroom while the custom-made chaise longue from Chair N Tango—a lifestyle company owned by the couple—offers a charming interlude to the inner sanctum.

left Danielle's passion for art in all its many facets initiated her design for the villa. The different layers and textures in the master bedroom ensure this space will remain timeless in its appeal.

right The custom-made vanity unit from Chair N Tango harks back to the heady and glamorous '30s and '40s. A piece of silk casually arranged on one wall adds texture and romance to the space.

living with art "The owners' contemporary Canadian artwork was so impressive, it was the most obvious and natural starting point," says the designer at kzdesigns of her approach to the interiors of this house in Singapore.

right "The soothing tones of the painting by Robert Christie inspired the color palette for the master bedroom. The clients wanted a room that had clean, almost masculine lines and this bed from Oser with leather headboard fit the bill," the designer says. Two rectangular standard lamps from Asiatique add height as well as definition to the space. Contrasting with the rectilinear nature of the bedroom is this round tortoiseshell plate from Club 21.

left "Often the hallway is dismissed as a mere conduit to another part of the house," the designer says. "But I saw this as a wonderful opportunity to direct the eye to this painting by William Perehudoff." The tenants gave this to each other as an anniversary present. "It started a trend and now we have bought other paintings for other anniversaries—better than jewelry," they say.

below The client's husband is a stereo buff and bought this system in Tokyo in 1977. "It is the opposites that give the room character," says the designer. The pastels of Robert Christie's painting contrast with the dark wood of the planter's chair and the strong masculine lines of the stereo system.

tribal tribute   Primitive art, bright colors, paintings and books are the passions cele-
brated in the exotic bedroom of Bangkok businessman Arthur Napolitano, resulting
in a unique style that is simultaneously modern and ethnic.

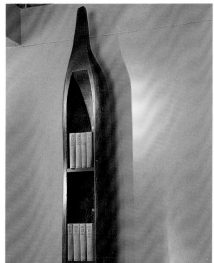

above Created by Design Plus, the bedroom is a tribute to the owner's travels and distinctive tastes. Matching Balinese doors lead to the children's rooms and were painted blue to contrast with the warm orange walls. The brick frames give the impression that the doors are outside the house, while adding an interesting texture to the wall. Balinese rice pounders of monumental size are used as décor elements along with an Afghan tribal rug.

left This quirky bookshelf is made from a fisherman's canoe brought from Lake Batur in Bali. The homeowner admired its sculptural look and fashioned it into a bookshelf to hold his collection of Joseph Conrad works.

opposite A Navajo serape from a Sotheby's auction in New York hangs above the floating platform bed draped with an Ashanti Kente textile from Ghana, matched with a Italian lamp shaped like an ice cube. The modern painting by Indonesian artist Krijono was bought in Bali.

sexy in the city The Bangkok cityscape silhouette visible from this bedroom in Siri Sathorn service apartments inspired Carolyn Corogin of C2 Studio to create a space that evokes the dazzling sophistication of life in an international metropolis.

above Elegant sliding doors give the option of enlarging the small sleeping space, so the bedroom can be both private sanctuary at night or part of the living room by day. Mirrors give the illusion of depth, while the long bolster and matching bench add horizontal elements to balance the vertical lines on the wall behind.

right Eschewing the typical bedroom layout with the headboard against the wall, the skyline is used as a three-dimensional headboard for a high-impact first impression. A soft duvet makes the service apartment more homey. The overall result is a plush and inviting city bedroom, a jewel in the sky.

old made new The classic Thai house, with its signature architectural and life-style elements, was the inspiration for this modern resort suite at Phuket Yacht Club, designed by Prinda Puranananda of Cowperthwaite & Puranananda Design.

left Thai architectural elements are seen in the sliding wooden doors, classic temple architrave, and the bed base, which mimics the base of a Thai stupa. The red–white pottery is a reproduction Ban Chiang artifact, and the reproduction bas relief, of the Thai Khmer style.

top and above The sliding doors open by day onto a brilliant sea view; by night they close to show a gold-leaf painting, easing the eye in place of boring curtains. The mosquito net is anchored on a wood carving like that found on the ceilings of Thai temples.

light fantastic For Han Loke Kwang of HYLA, who designed this Singapore house, one of the things he loves best about the master bedroom is the "open relationship between the bedroom and the bathroom, each making the other more interesting."

above The sliding timber louvers and cantilevered roof give the bedroom a tree house feel.
below right These accessories from Lifestorey accentuate the rust and orange color tones used in the room.
left The main features of the room are transparency and neatness of design. The wall doubles as headboard, concealing the wardrobe, and houses these unusual air-conditioning vents from Japan. The clothes horse and two white vases from X•TRA Living introduce a very modern element to the room.

purple reigns The purity of the overall whiteness exudes serenity while dashes of purple add soul to the master bedroom in this house in Singapore designed by Sim Boon Yang of Eco-id Architects.

above "Purple is our favorite color," says the owner. The different sizes and shapes of these cushions from The Link and Quedos augment the purple silk lap throw the owner had purchased "from a French lady who designed and made soft furnishings in Shanghai."

left One of the growing trends in Asian bedrooms is to eschew the use of headboards. Here, the master bedroom and bathroom form one continuous space separated only by the dividing wall that acts as support for the bed. The room is imbued with natural light which adds to the airiness of the room. A simple low bench that runs the length of the wall is perfect for the television and as a display unit for these vases from The Touch.

below Having an easy chair in the bedroom is a must and this Attendo chair designed by Peter Maly for COR at Marquis is a stylish choice.

taking center stage Opulence of space is the hallmark of this master bedroom in Deanna Birch's Singapore home designed by the Italian team Sottsass Associati. The sloping ceiling directs the eye to the enormous, centrally placed bed.

right The low windows, covering an entire wall, are ideally suited to the space and allow oodles of light to enter the room. In accordance with the strict regulations regarding child safety however, a barrier had to be erected in front of the windows. The architect has made a creative feature of the obligatory grille with these stylish white bars. A lacquer pot from Vietnam, given to Deanna by a close friend, makes for a stylish embellishment.

left A large bedroom might presuppose creating spaces within spaces. Deanna, however, has opted to showcase the magnificent bed. The headboard is 17th century Chinese rosewood, and the mattress is an American waterbed, fashioned from 18 tightly compacted tubes of water. She also wanted bedside tables that would not distract from the transparency of the room, and had these glass-topped cane tables made locally. Another feature of the bed is that it doubles as a dressing screen, while the simple reading lamps from IKEA provide a pleasing contrast to the antique pieces. When it came to the color for the room, burgundy was a natural choice. "I love burgundy," Deanna says. "It goes with all shades of wood." A richly patterned rug from Pakistan adds the finishing touch.

below right Complementing the headboard and the pale wood of the wardrobe are these intricately carved 19th century clothes hangers Deanna found in Guangzhou.

splendor in the gray The growing trend in many Asian properties is for spacious bedrooms that make a definitive statement as illustrated here in the master bedroom of a Singapore apartment designed by Sim Boon Yang of Eco-id Architects.

above The monastic air of this guest bedroom is relieved by the captivating ensemble of antiques and artifacts collected on the owners' many travels. Ralph Lauren bed linen and pillows from Princess and the Pea are juxtaposed with this unusual tile rug, a hanging basket from Laos and camel saddle from Saudi Arabia.

right There is a distinctive quality about gray that rarely goes out of fashion. Thai silk panels that compose the back wall add a quiet elegance to the master bedroom. The custom-made bed and bedside tables are understated but eye-catching. White details like the Flos lamps and Erik Jørgensen chair from X•TRA add the modern dimension.

hideaway haven The pool villas at Evason Resort & Spa in Hua Hin, Thailand, are conceived as a self-contained world within a world, with a bedroom suite, private pool and outdoor bathroom and lotus pond enclosed within wooden walls.

above A light, bright color palette keeps the mood fresh and relaxing. Blonde wood furnishings have the casual rustic look that matches a beach resort. This chair has simple geometric lines that give it a young, yet timeless look that never goes out of style.

left More for show than for functional use in the air-conditioned room, the soft white mosquito netting is an ode to tropical style, lending dreamy romance to the hotel room. A good night's sleep is ensured with a plump bed layered with fat pillows and a fluffy duvet.

top Pretty and practical, the sitting area consists of a day bed. Covered with cushions by day, it's a sofa; tucked with sheets at night it becomes an extra bed. Built-in drawers provide extra storage space.

above Instead of a boxy four-poster bed, the mosquito net hangs from a simple but stylish frame made of bamboo poles suspended from the ceiling.

dreaming in red   When is a bedroom more than just a crash pad? When it is the bedrooms at Downtown Apartments in Bali designed by the Nine Squares design team and kitted out with all the trappings of modern indulgence.

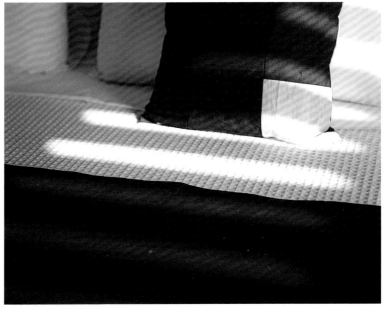

above The initial impression of precise and emphatic lines in this bedroom is given an unexpected twist by the introduction of decadent details such as the suede headboard, plush red cushions and bedspread and the provocative artwork.

left This white plastic fan introduces an irreverently quirky touch to the rooms.

opposite Veronique Aonzo's dramatic artwork has a definite rock star appeal. The layering of textures like the gray suede headboard, leather cushions, brick light boxes and crimson roses on the marble bedside tables add an idiosyncratic sumptuousness to the space.

balinese reveries When it came to designing Villa Ylang Ylang in Bali for herself and her husband Mike, Danielle Mahon's objective was to create a romantic and sensual environment in the bedrooms.

above Danielle opted for basic black, cream and white with touches of warm gold and natural dark finishes for the guest bedroom. The sleigh-like beds draped in muslin have a fairytale quality to them. As her husband Mike is involved in high fashion, he has collected a variety of fabrics from Valentino, Versace and Armani over the years. Danielle put these to good use for the soft furnishings in the room.

right It is not unusual for bathrooms in Bali to be open to the elements. However, Danielle has introduced a romantic twist in her design by hanging gossamer-thin curtains and big lounging cushions at the entrance to the bathroom. In this way, the boudoir feel of the room is extended to the exterior. Black and white terrazzo in the sunken bath and mother-of-pearl inlay add a wistful touch.

resort in the sky Inspired by tropical resorts, the owners of this Bangkok penthouse incorporated an outdoor bathroom suite, screened from neighboring buildings with a wooden lattice and plants, into their highrise master bedroom.

left The contemporary B&B Italia bed and Ligne Roset sofa share the room with the owner's collection of Asian antiques, such as this 19th century black lacquer Chinese cabinets displaying a pair of Khmer figurines.

above Above the black Chinese antique bench, a glass wall panel slides back so that the bathtub becomes part of the room. A fiery glow comes from the iron and gold-leaf interiors of the lamps by Catelonni and Smith.

art from the heart   When Philip Lakeman and Graham Oldroyd designed their
Bali villa, it developed "out of a sense of wanting an elegant minimal space that
had a proportion of parts which made visual sense to us as artists."

above The artists' home is filled with their idiosyncratic artwork such as these models from their quirky hound collection.
top left The bold reds and gold of this painting add depth and glamor to the room.
left Behind the bed is this striking concrete console table.

left The open plan of the pavilions that form the villa allows views into and out of the room. The interior and exterior spaces merge seamlessly into one. The artists' "Love" collage (far right) makes for an engrossing story especially when paired with the kitschy but cool larva lamp.

understated luxury While some clients might decide on a more neutral palette for their bedrooms, in this house in Singapore designed by Kevin Tan of aKTa-rchitects, the owners have instead opted for a style that is pure opulence.

left The appeal of this master bedroom is in its different stages. At the entrance is a lift which gives onto a walk-in wardrobe which in turn leads into the bedroom proper. Apart from the raised bed with silk headboard, the room is devoted to art, from the dramatic painting above the bed to the array of antique white porcelain vases and delicate pottery arranged in cabinets around the room.

above Whereas the rest of the room concentrates on classical artwork, this corner of the room is super-modern with these iconic lights from Million Lighting and streamlined armchairs. Heavy silk drapes add to the room's air of quiet contemplation.

modern classic The timeless appeal of muted tones in the bedroom of this Singapore apartment, designed by Calvin Sim and Lim Siew Hui of Eco-id Architects and Design Consultancy, appeals to a clientele wanting the ultimate in luxe living.

right "I did not want the room design to distract from the great view outside," says Lim Siew Hui. The modern classic design concept is both sophisticated and elegant with the accent on custom-made furniture. A large canvas in burnished gold by Sim Kern Teck dominates one wall.
left A standard lamp from Million Lighting and custom-made mirror and console by Hugues Chevalier create a perfect symmetry in the master bedroom.
below left The organic shape of this Flos table lamp is mirrored in a vase filled with soft, delicate rose heads.

room to spare An extra room can always serve double duty as a guest room and study, like this glamorous bedroom in Bangkok designed for Domus condominiums by Singaporean design firm APC.

above This sleek, black leather office chair and Italian lamp show how the right color can make a simple work desk look sexy.
left Wall-length curtains are made from sliding fabric panels, so the shiny fabric hangs flat for a sleek, sharp line. The synthetic fabric mimics the shimmer of silk but is easier to maintain. A white, shaggy rug and fuzzy cushions from Fabrio add softness, balancing the shiny textures.

blonde bedroom Furnishing is kept to the bare minimum in this bedroom designed by DWP Cityspace for Sky Villas in Bangkok, allowing the glow of the vanilla and natural materials to fill the space with their warm, earthy appeal.

left Layers of cushions provide couch-like comfort for watching the flat-screen TV mounted on the facing wall.

below This curved wooden sculpture is actually a funky rocking stool.

right With only a bed, night-stands and a stool, the floor is kept bare to showcase the beauty of the bamboo-patterned wood flooring. Organic texture is provided by the woven hemp wall covering, and the faux fur throw adds a touch of luxury.

bath convertible   This master bedroom and bathroom suite created by Singaporean firm APC for Domus condominiums in Bangkok shows one interpretation of how the open bath makes a space bigger, giving a greater sense of luxurious personal space.

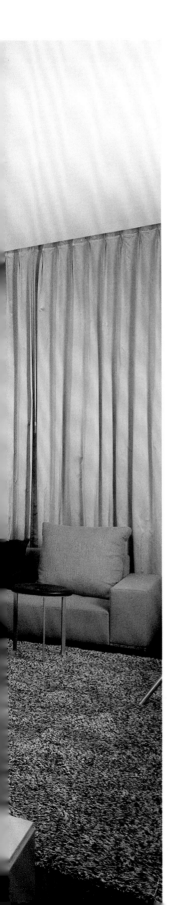

above The sliding wood panel
is both bathroom wall and door.
Beside the tub, the frosted glass
shower stall will reveal the sexy
silhouette of the bather within.
left Sliding wood panels give
the option of an open or closed
bathroom—you can soak in the
tub while watching TV in the
next room! The Minotti bed is a
bed, headboard and nightstands
in a single unit. Dressed up with
jumbo-sized Minotti cushions, a
sumptuous silk throw from Jim
Thompson and Artimede bedside
lamps, it contains all the comforts
needed for reading and watching TV in bed.

asian mystique Contemporary Asian luxe is the look in this guest room in Golden Nakara villas designed by the Bangkok firm P49 Deesign. The deep green and purple palette gives an exotic depth to the simple furnishings.

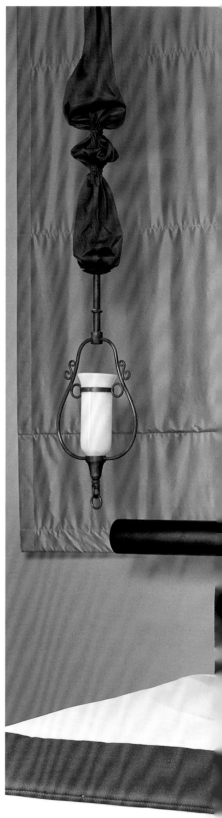

above This sofa is really a big day bed with jumbo cushioning for sofa support. A twin theme in the color and furnishings gives balance—the sofa has room enough for two. Matching desks and mirrors can be both desk and vanity counter.

right The upholstered head-board gives sofa-like backing, enhanced by layers of cushions. Synthetic fabric gives the silken shimmer of luxury and offers easy maintenance. Hanging lamps leave plenty of space on the night tables beneath.

above Low-slung and long, this creamy chair is meant for laid back lounging.

right The subtle, tawny palette gives lulling warmth that's conducive to slumber. An elegant headboard adds drama and style to even the simplest room. The soft fabric headboard adds the illusion of height. Heaps of petite cushions and a mini bolster piled on a creamy bedspread lend an appealing feminine touch to the neutral background.

biscuit and cream   Barely-there color in natural, neutral tones is the uniform of today's understated bedroom, as seen in this guest room designed by Leo Design for Golden Nakara villas in Bangkok.

the modern monastic The sheer simplicity of this zen-style bedroom created by Index Design at The Equatorial in Singapore lies in the clean lines and minimal accessories ensuring a restful and harmonious experience.

above Even in a relatively small space like this, a bedroom can function equally well as a place for retiring and as a cozy office. **left** The main point of interest in this bedroom is the simple but effective floor-to-ceiling spray-painted ply wall panel. Shades of blues and browns add a masculinity to the room while the ledge is a modern take on the Victorian picture rails.

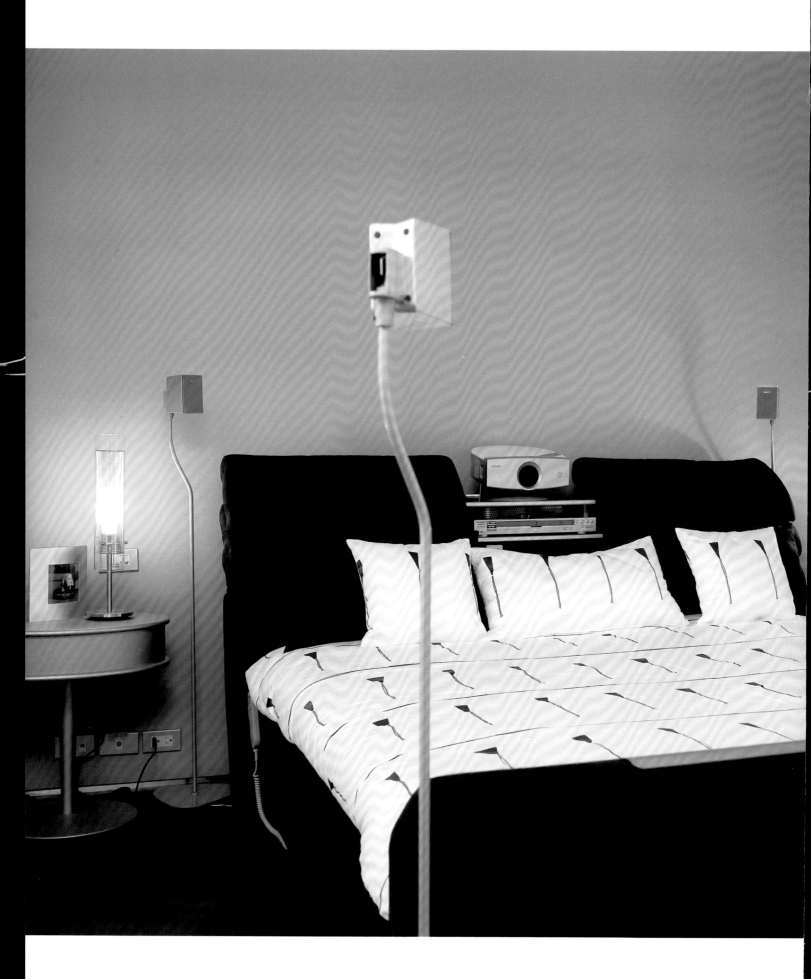

private screening Today's bedrooms seem incomplete without the ubiquitous TV for bedtime channel surfing, like this Bangkok bedroom designed by DWP Cityspace for Sky Villas with an oh-so-indulgent bed-cum-movie theater.

left The high-tech bed is invitingly covered in soft faux suede, and has an adjustable headboard with a variety of reclining options that transforms the bed into a bigger and better sofa for optimal movie viewing.

above Private screenings come at the touch of a fingertip, giving hours of lazy amusement for die-hard film fanatics. Seen from the bathroom's frosted glass double sliding doors, the screen emerges from the foot of the bed. Leather floor tiles are a treat for bare feet, while a shaggy white rug adds an extra layer of luxury.

sheer romance   The mosquito net endures as a timeless décor feature that adds wispy romance to any room. It's like icing on a cake in this master bedroom designed by Abacus Design for Sky Villas condominiums in Bangkok.

above The bathroom with footed tub, twin basins and dramatic black marble brings hotel-like luxury into the home.

left With a sumptuous en suite bathroom of hotel proportions, this style appeals to up-and-coming urban executives who like things lavish. The glamor of gold is unleashed with generous abandon in this master bedroom. The headboard wall is covered in a matte gold fabric that is echoed in the curtains. Gold shimmer comes from the bolster and cushions. Elements of Thai style appear in the classic carving above the bed, and the wallpaper with the gold-leaf effect.

right No space is wasted. A structural pillar creates an awkward alcove. Fitted with a ledge, it instantly becomes a desk and personal study area, with a cityscape view to boot!

a quiet comfort Designed by Peter Tiong of the Singaporean firm APC, the all-white interiors at the Twin Palms Phuket resort create an understated, non-impact effect "because we go to resorts for peace and quiet, not loudness."

left "You may not remember the room, but you take away the overall experience of comfort and relaxation," says the designer. Dark wood and white walls give the tropical Asian feeling, while sliding doors—which are a particularly Asian element—are used as bathroom walls.

above The white color scheme creates a pure, simple space. The room is "a quiet layering of comfortable things"—soft pillows, roomy bed, ambient lighting.

right The geometric furnishings echo the square-shaped room. The square furnishings conform to the scale and proportion of the room so the lines blend and don't distract the eye.

indulging in personal kneads The bedroom spa, inspired by the region's many luxury spas, is the latest Asian trend. A fabulous personal massage room is the highlight of this master suite created by P49 Deesign for Bangkok's Golden Nakara villas.

left The room's contemporary classic elegance is embodied in this four-poster bed romantically swathed in diaphanous drapes that are not exactly mosquito netting, but suggest the idea of it. The high ceiling uses layers of cove lighting which bounces the light back upwards, softening the light in the room.

right An antechamber between bedroom and bathroom serves as a spa and dressing room, complete with a massage table, towel rack and scented oils within arm's reach. One of the closet doors cleverly conceals a built-in sauna.

below A sliding panel opens a flow space between bedroom and bathroom. The mirror is fixed on poles so as to give a free-floating effect.

plush platform   Grown-up glamor is the high-impact effect of this plush master bedroom designed by Leo Design for Golden Nakara villas in Bangkok. The effect is like a sumptuous hotel suite for the serious executive.

left This suite consists of a vast bedroom with equally enormous dressing room and bathroom, which includes a large peek-a-boo window looking into the bedroom. The bed is the star of the show, located on a carpeted platform and elegantly framed by an upholstered headboard. With no sharp lines or hard surfaces, all the furnishing are covered in thick, soft materials in muted tones, creating a luxurious bedroom that invites the occupant to sink into its plushness.
right The curving, sensuous lines of this Art Deco chair bring retro style to the 21st century.
below The bed is the new sofa, hence "plump" and "fuzzy" have become the key buzzwords defining modern cushion looks.

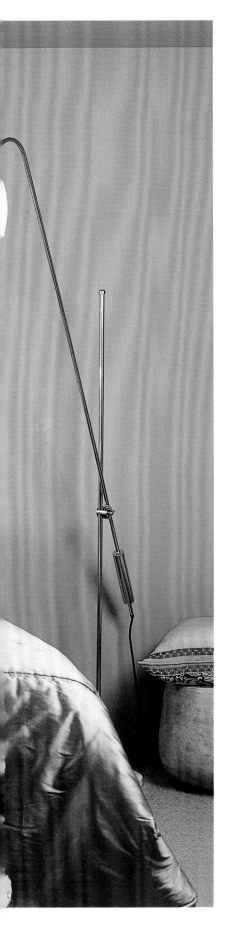

modishly eclectic Today's bedrooms offer more than just spaces to sleep in. At the Vanilla Home showroom in Singapore, this bedroom, styled by kzdesigns, is part bohemian studio and part celebration of classic contemporary design.

left An eggshell blue wall offers the perfect backdrop for Irene Hauger's "Pumpkin" painting. The two Task lamps introduce an urban industrial feel while the Pamela Tang silk bedspread and Fortuny velvet cushions add a rich sensuality.

above Irene Hauger's "Snow Branches" sets the mood in this corner of the bedroom where Vanilla Home's limestone and wrought-iron table acts as a display area for Lesli Berggren's jewelry. The svelte silver-plated vases and candlestick by Lambert contrast well with the Fortuny velvet cushions.

left Fur is the ultimate in luxurious abandonment. The various elements in this bedroom each offer a different tactile experience. Jim Thomson silk and Pierre Frey faux fur for the headboard is a winning combination. The silk component is continued in the bedspread and wrapped bedside tables. Highly individual snail fossil lamps balance the space. The marmotte throw on the bed is pure indulgence.

above Nicholas Haslam's campaign folding chair and cherry wood and leather travel desk have that certain "days of the Raj" quality about them and bring an extra dimension to the bedroom-cum-writing den. Fortuny's Cesendello floor lamp is simply exquisite.

high style at i.style With its clear-cut and simple lines, the master bedroom showcased at *i.Style living* in Singapore is proof that the modern and minimalist look is still very much in vogue in Asian homes.

above With its sleek aluminum base, this elegant day bed from Italian design company Ycami makes a stylish statement. The clever combination of polyester and canvas used for the cushion and bolsters is both silky and eminently durable.

left MisuraEmme has long been synonymous with design innovation as illustrated by this Tao platform bed with in-built asymmetric lights. The contrast between the natural oak finish of the bed with its brown and orange bed linen and the aluminum wardrobe is inspired and stylish.

right Minimize the wardrobe space with this chic aluminum MisuraEmme coat hanger and accessories box.

where the city never sleeps At the Mod.Living showroom in Singapore, designed by Woha Architects, this cosmopolitan bedroom encapsulates the individual and highly discerning spirit of contemporary living.

left Singapore's dynamic cityscape is a fitting backdrop for this state-of-the-art, supremely desirable bedroom. Every piece of furniture here is remarkable in its design concept and, with clean and unexpected lines make for unconventional and unmistakable statements.

right Susie MacMurray's balloon sculpture can be used as a rug, cushion or simply a gorgeous *objet d'art*.

below right Designed in 1990, Tom Dixon's Bird lounger for Cappellini is still considered a work of pure genius.

bottom The Oblio stool by Von Robinson for Moroso will strike an original note in any bedroom whether used for practical purposes or as an eye-catching sculpture. The soft fabric seat contrasts yet complements the rounded, space-age base.

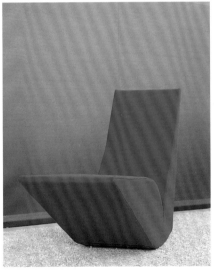

above The raised cream felt strips make this Molteni & C cushion one of a kind—soft enough to lie on and individual enough to please even the most discerning homeowner.

left Dark soothing tones rarely go out of fashion and this classic bedroom at Mod.Living is no exception. The Molteni & C glass-fronted wardrobe is the perfect backdrop for the Carlo Colombo bed for Cappellini Segno and the organic contours of Patrick Norguet's chair for Cappellini. Enrique Castanon's painting entitled "Panic" injects a burst of color.

mirror mirror When it came to this bedroom at The Equatorial in Singapore, the main consideration for the team at Index Design was that it should function as a "tranquil resting place" but one that was not "deemed boring."

right This dark wood console is an interesting approach to a vanity unit. Keeping to a simple design of white and dark wood heightens the illusion of space.
left Floor-to-ceiling leather paneling that doubles as headboard, and textured cushions "bring out the animal in you!" according to the creative team at Index Design.

shades of gray In spite of the relatively small size of this bedroom at The Equatorial in Singapore, the team at Index Design has managed to create a highrise miniature oasis that is both comfortable and stylish.

above The contrasting textures of silk and wool used in these customized cushions from Osborne and Little introduce a chic footnote against the crisp white bed linen.

left With its timeless elegance, gray is increasingly the color of choice for many designers whether in a living room or in a bedroom such as this one. Matched with dark wood and sheer drapes, it creates the impression of added space and has a clean, minimal feel to it. Soft pink flowers add a feminine touch.

electric blue is bliss Small spaces need not pose a barrier to creativity as Index Design proves with this ultra-stylish bedroom at The Equatorial in Singapore where brilliant blue makes for a bold and imaginative choice.

above The audacious use of brilliant blue in the bedspread and cushions from Osborne and Little make for a refreshing statement in the bedroom.
left The beauty of this room lies in the deft coordination of two main colors—bright blue and soft creams. A timber mosaic panel behind the bed lays the groundwork for the geometry in the rest of the room echoed in the roman blinds, window ledge that doubles as a display unit, as well as the dark wood console and stool.

The authors would like to express their thanks to the following people who gave their kind support during the production of this book:

BALI
Arthur Chondros at Downtown Apartments, Jose Luis Calle at The Balé, Jaya Ibrahim, Anjarini Kencahyati, Philip Lakeman and Graham Oldroyd, Antony Liu, Mike and Danielle Mahon, Hansjörg Meier at The Legian, Daniel Ellaway of Nine Squares, Richard North-Lewis of Stoneworks, Shinta Siregar of Nexus Studio Architects, Fredo Taffin of Espace Concept and Gill Wilson.

Antony Liu Budiwihardja Jl Raya Perjuangan, Kompleks Plaza Kebun, Jeruk Blok E-11, Jakarta Barat 11530, tel: (62) 021 535 0319/25/34, email: tonton@dnet.net.id

Fredo Taffin Espace Concept, 250 Beddington Rd, Noosa Heads Doonan 4562, Queensland Australia, www.espaceconcept.net

Jaya Pratomo Ibrahim email: jayaibrahim@jaya-associates.com

Nexus Studio Architects Perkantoran Duta Wijaya, Unit 1, Jl Raya Puputan, Denpasar, Bali, tel: (62) 361 744 3493, email: nexus@dps.centrin.net.id

Nine Squares email: info@ninesquares.com, www.ninesquares.com

Pesamuan Jln Pungutan 25, Sanur Bali, www.pesamuan-bali.com

Veronique Aonzo email: mymonamour@hotmail.com

SINGAPORE
Kevin Tan of aKTa-rchitects, Albano Daminato, Sim Boon Yang, Calvin Sim and Lim Siew Hui of Eco-id Architects and Design Consultancy, Han Loke Kwang and Hilary Lo of HYLA Architects, Angelena Chan and Fiona Ng of Index Design, staff at *i.Style living*, Geraldine Archer of MARA MIRI, staff at Mod.Living and Stefanie Hauger and Rebecca Metcalfe at Vanilla Home.

Albano Daminato Design and Interior Architecture, Robinson Rd PO Box 1267, S'pore 902517, tel: (65) 9630 8482, email: albano@pacific.net.sg

Ann Healey www.annhealey.com

aKTa-rchitects 25 Seah St #05-01, S'pore 188381, tel: (65) 63334331, www.akta.com.sg

Asiatique Collections Blk 14-5, Dempsey Rd, S'pore 249675, tel: (65) 6471 3146, email: asiatiq8@singnet.com.sg

Club 21 Gallery Four Seasons Hotel, #01-07/8, 190 Orchard Blvd, S'pore 248646, tel: (65) 6887 5451, www.clubtwentyone.com

Eco-id Architects & Design Consultancy 11 Stamford Rd, #04-06, Capitol Bldg, S'pore 178884, tel: (65) 6337 5119, email: ecoid@pacific.net.sg

Flos www.flos.net

HYLA Architects 47 Ann Siang Rd #02-01, S'pore 069720, tel: (65) 6324 2488, www.hyla.com.sg

Index Design 15-A Purvis St, S'pore 188594, tel: (65) 6220 1002, fax: (65) 6334 7262

i.Style living 101 Thomson Rd, #02-22/27 United Square, S'pore 307591, tel: (65) 6352 7727, www.istyleliving.com.sg

kzdesigns tel/fax: (65) 6836 3365, email: rokasing@singnet.com.sg, www.kzdesigns.com

Lifestorey Great World City #02-33D, 1 Kim Seng Parade, S'pore 237994, tel: (65) 6732 7362, www.lifestorey.com

MARA MIRI email: gnrptltd@singnet.com.sg

Marquis Furniture Gallery 1 Kim Seng Parade, #02-33D Great World City, S'pore 237994, tel: (65) 6732 7362, www.marquis.com.sg

Million Electric Co 11 Kallang Way 5, Kolam Ayer Industrial Park, S'pore 349030, tel : (65) 6743 3033, www.millionlighting.com.sg

Mod.Living 331 North Bridge Rd, #02-01/08 Odeon Towers, S'pore 188720, tel: (65) 6336 2286, www.modliving.com.sg

Oser Design 25 Seah St #02-01, S'pore 188381, tel: (65) 6336 2002, www.oser.com.sg

Princess and the Pea 129 Devonshire Rd, S'pore 239886, tel: (65) 6275 6345, www.princessonline.net

Quedos Home Works 61 Stamford Rd, #01-02 Stamford Court, S'pore 178892, tel: (65) 6338 1171, www.quedoshomeworks.com

Sottsass Associati www.sottsass.it

The Link Boutique # 01-10 Palais Renaissance, 390 Orchard Rd, S'pore 238871, tel: (65) 6737 7503, www.TheLink.com.sg

The Touch House of Art and Design 38 Bukit Pasoh Rd, S'pore 089852, tel: (65) 6325 4990, www.thetouch.com.sg

Vanilla Home 48 Club St, S'pore 069425, tel: (65) 6324 6206, fax: (65) 6324 6207

X·TRA Living 9 Penang Rd, #02-01 Park Mall, S'pore 238459, tel: (65) 6339 4664, www.xtra.com.sg

Woha Architects 175 Telok Ayer St, S'pore 068623, tel: (65) 6423 4555, www.wohadesigns.com

THAILAND
Carolyn Corogin of C2 Studio, Rika Dila, Vichien Chansevikul, Michael Palmer, Raymond Eaton, Arthur Napolitano, Brian Renaud, H Ernest Lee, Eva Malmstrom-Shivdasani, Jacques Baume, Sylvain Guisetti, Laura Herne of Outlaurs, Nusra Kongsujarit and Kessiri Loilawa of Challenge Property, Delia Oakins of Carpediem Galleries, Nuchareekorn Kornkirati of The Sukhothai Bangkok, Kingkaew Puengjesada and Kittima Kritiyachotipakorn of Golden Land Property, Debbie Thio and Supranee Taecharungroj of The Metropolitan Bangkok, Olivier Gibaud of Twin Palms Phuket and Uracha Jaktaranon of 124 Communications.

Abacus Design 144 Soi Siripot, Sukhumvit 81, Bangkok 10250, tel: (662) 742 457 16/331 9966, fax: (662) 332 8649, email: abacus@ji-net.com

C2 Studio The Prime Bldg, Level 15, Suites B&C, 24 Sukhumvit 21, Bangkok 10110, tel: (662) 260 4243, fax: (662) 260 4316, email: Carolyn@c2studio.net

Carpediem Galleries #1B-1 Ruam Rudee Bldg, 566 Ploenchit Rd, Bangkok 10330, tel: (662) 250 0408, fax: (662) 250 0409, email: deliaok@loxinfo.co.th

Domus (sales office) 18th Floor Lake Rajada Complex, 193/72 Rajadapisek Rd, Bangkok 10110, tel: (662) 661 9300, fax: (662) 661 9331, email: bkk_res-sales@cbre.com, www.domus.co.th

DWP Cityspace The Dusit Thani Bldg, Level 11, 946 Rama 4 Rd, Bangkok 10550, tel: (662) 267 3939, fax: (662) 267 3949, email: nijaya.i@dwpartnership.com, www.dwpartnership.com

Golden Nakara Golden Land Property Development, 8th Floor, Golden Bldg, 153/3 Soi Mahardlekluang 1, Rajdamri Rd, Bangkok 10330, tel: (662) 652 1111, fax: (662) 652 1511, www.goldenlandplc.com

IAW Soi Panich-Anan Sukhumvit 71, Bangkok 10110, tel: (662) 713 1237, fax: (662) 713 1238, email: iawbkk@loxinfo.co.th

The Metropolitan Bangkok 27 South Sathorn Rd, Bangkok 10120, tel: (662) 625 3333, fax: (662) 625 3300, email: info.bkk@metropolitan.como.bz, www.metropolitan.como.bz

Leo Design 555 SSP Tower, 10th Floor, Sukhumvit Soi 63, Ekamai Rd, Bangkok, tel: (662) 381 6363 7, fax: (662) 381 6368

P49 Deesign 74 Soi Langsuan, Ploenchit Rd, Bangkok 10330, tel: (662) 652 290 015, fax: (662) 652 2200

Sky Villas The Ascott Bangkok, 187 South Sathorn Rd, Bangkok 10120, Thailand, tel: (662) 676 8888, www.goldenlandplc.com

State Tower Challenge Property Co 1055/111 State Tower Bangkok, Silom Rd, Bangkok 10500, tel: (662) 630 8888, fax: (662) 630 5609, www.challenge.co.th

The Sukhothai Bangkok 13/3 South Sathorn Rd, Bangkok 10120, tel: (662) 287 0222, fax: (662) 287 4980, www.sukhothai.com